THINKING THROUGH COMPREHENSION

Written by Gunter Schymkiw

Published by Prim-Ed Publishing

www.prim-ed.com

0239C

24/2

THINKING SKILLS THROUGH COMPREHENSION *(Upper)*

Published by R.I.C. Publications® 2002

Reprinted under licence by
Prim-Ed Publishing 2006

Copyright© Gunter Schymkiw 2002

ISBN 1 84654 029 1

PR–0239

Additional titles available in this series:
THINKING SKILLS THROUGH COMPREHENSION *(Middle)*

Offices in: Bosheen, New Ross, Co. Wexford, Ireland

Email: sales@prim-ed.com

Internet websites

In some cases, websites or specific URLs may be recommended. While these are checked and rechecked at the time of publication, the publisher has no control over any subsequent changes which may be made to webpages. It is *strongly* recommended that the class teacher checks *all* URLs before allowing students to access them.

View all pages online

http://www.prim-ed.com

Prim-Ed Publishing   www.prim-ed.com

Foreword

The *Thinking skills through comprehension* series offers pupils opportunities to think critically, logically and creatively to solve problems.

Each problem-solving activity is in the context of a short mystery story which pupils should find both challenging and stimulating as they are put in the situation of being a detective whose task is to solve a crime.

To do this they must gather information by responding accurately to a series of text-related questions. From the information collected they are required to make connections and draw logical conclusions to solve each short mystery.

While the main focus of the activities is thinking logically or creatively within the literary framework, various other learning areas are covered.

Pupils will respond with enthusiasm to the challenges presented to them in this book.

Also available in this series:

Thinking skills through comprehension (Middle)

Contents

Teachers Notes

Prim-Ed Publishing   www.prim-ed.com

The mystery story genre is a favourite of fiction. The *Thinking skills through comprehension* series provides pupils with a broad range of comprehension and critical thinking activities.

The major questioning types and styles of thinking addressed by this book include:

Literal –   Recognising related information in text.

Evaluative –   Making judgments using own opinions or related to defined standards.

Analysis –   Thinking critically. Examining the components of a text or scenario.

Making inferences.

Drawing conclusions.

Synthesis –   Reorganising information to examine alternative possibilities.

Page 1 provides a fun introduction to the style of activities in the book.

The remainder of the book consists of two-page activities. The main focus of the activities are for the pupils to think critically, logically and creatively to solve problems.

A stimulating story challenges pupils to take on a role of a 'detective' whose job it is to solve a 'mystery'.

To achieve a solution, pupils must gather information by responding accurately to a series of text-related questions.

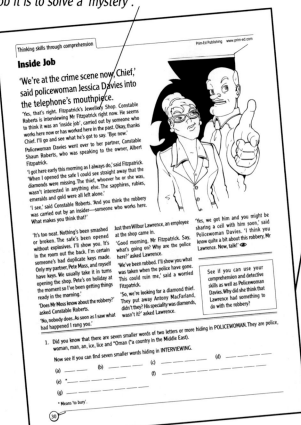

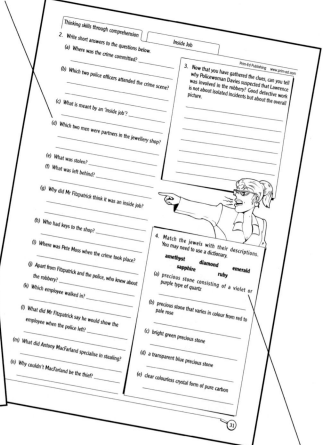

Literal questioning plays a large part in this process. Like good detectives, pupils must then use evaluative and inferential techniques to analyse this information. From this analysis they are asked to offer a plausible solution to the mystery.

Prim-Ed Publishing   www.prim-ed.com

Curriculum Links

Country	Subject	Age/Level	Objectives
England	English (Reading)	KS 2	• understand texts by using inference and deduction, looking for meaning beyond the literal, making connections between different parts of a text and using their knowledge of other texts read • read for information by scanning texts to find information, obtaining specific information through detailed reading and considering an argument critically
Northern Ireland	English (Reading)	KS 2	• read a range of stories • read for information • interpret texts read • justify responses to text by using inference, deduction and by referring to evidence within the text • learn that different reading purposes require a variety of reading skills; e.g. recalling and scanning
Republic of Ireland	English (Reading)	5th/6th Class	• engage with an increasing range of narrative text • read a more challenging range of reading material • use comprehension skills • develop study skills such as scanning and summarising • support arguments and opinions with evidence from the text
Scotland	English (Reading)	D	• encounter fiction texts of some complexity • discuss main ideas of texts and make predictions about them • consider facts and weighing of evidence to decide whether an argument is valid
		E	• read, understand and select relevant information in order to solve problems • evaluate, infer and make judgements about texts
Wales	English (Reading)	KS 2	• read for information, using progressively more challenging and demanding texts • read texts with challenging subject matter that extend thinking • use inference, deduction and prediction to evaluate texts they read • refer to relevant passages to support their opinions • read for different purposes, including scanning to locate information and detailed reading to obtain specific information • use dictionaries to explain unfamiliar vocabulary

Skills Overview

Prim-Ed Publishing   www.prim-ed.com

Pupils who successfully complete the activities in this book will have demonstrated the following skills:

Skill	Think and Save Ink Page 1	Why Did He Get the Sack? Pages 2–3	It's All in My Book Pages 4–5	The Great Train (Robbery) Mess Up Pages 6–7	The Rich Man's Lawns Pages 8–9	The Great Escape Pages 10–11	The Insurance Claim Pages 12–13	Charming Beauregarde Pages 14–15	Where's The Heir? Pages 16–17	Nuisance Call Pages 18–19	Innocent Or Guilty? Pages 20–21
locate information in a text		✧	✧	✧	✧	✧	✧	✧	✧	✧	✧
answer literal questions		✧	✧	✧	✧	✧	✧	✧	✧	✧	✧
use critical thinking to analyse text and solve problems		✧	✧	✧	✧	✧	✧	✧	✧	✧	✧
synthesise information to formulate solutions	✧	✧	✧			✧			✧	✧	
evaluate information and make logical judgments based on this evaluation		✧	✧	✧	✧	✧	✧	✧	✧	✧	✧
apply knowledge to assist in problem solving		✧	✧	✧	✧	✧	✧		✧	✧	✧
use technical knowledge to assist in problem solving			✧	✧			✧			✧	✧
use context clues to find word meanings		✧	✧	✧	✧						
locate information using a variety of reference tools		✧	✧	✧	✧	✧		✧		✧	✧
draw inferences to make generalisations about a text		✧	✧		✧	✧		✧	✧		✧
use a dictionary to find the meaning of unknown words		✧		✧	✧	✧		✧	✧	✧	✧
draw on a personal experience to make observations					✧				✧	✧	
manipulate sounds in words to solve puzzles				✧		✧	✧				
sequence events logically in a text											
apply understandings at a creative interpersonal level		✧			✧						
use homonyms									✧		
make illustrations											
reflect personally on a text											
link words to their synonyms		✧									
examine ideas critically from different perspectives		✧				✧			✧	✧	✧
make associations				✧	✧		✧	✧	✧		
complete a cloze activity			✧								
write to support a particular point of view		✧	✧	✧	✧	✧	✧	✧	✧	✧	✧

Skills Overview

Prim-Ed Publishing   www.prim-ed.com

Pupils who successfully complete the activities in this book will have demonstrated the following skills:

Skill	The Jilted Lover Pages 22 – 23	Happy Holidays Pages 24 – 25	The Kidnapped Kidnapper Pages 26 – 27	Sir Marvo The Dull Pages 28 – 29	Inside Job Pages 30 – 31	Crooks Never Prosper Pages 32 – 33	Late Again Pages 34 – 35	Bad Day For Bobby Pages 36 – 37
locate information in a text	✦	✦	✦	✦	✦	✦	✦	✦
answer literal questions	✦	✦	✦	✦	✦	✦	✦	✦
use critical thinking to analyse text and solve problems	✦	✦	✦	✦	✦	✦	✦	✦
synthesise information to formulate solutions	✦	✦		✦	✦	✦	✦	✦
evaluate information and make logical judgments based on this evaluation	✦	✦	✦	✦	✦	✦	✦	✦
apply knowledge to assist in problem solving	✦	✦	✦	✦	✦	✦	✦	✦
use technical knowledge to assist in problem solving	✦	✦		✦				
use context clues to find word meanings		✦						
locate information using a variety of reference tools	✦	✦	✦	✦	✦		✦	
draw inferences to make generalisations about a text	✦	✦	✦	✦	✦	✦	✦	
use a dictionary to find the meaning of unknown words	✦	✦		✦	✦		✦	
draw on a personal experience to make observations	✦	✦	✦	✦	✦	✦	✦	✦
manipulate sounds in words to solve puzzles				✦	✦			
sequence events logically in a text		✦		✦	✦	✦		✦
apply understandings at a creative interpersonal level						✦		
use homonyms								
make illustrations								✦
reflect personally on a text			✦				✦	
link words to their synonyms							✦	
examine ideas critically from different perspectives		✦	✦	✦	✦	✦	✦	✦
make associations	✦	✦		✦	✦	✦	✦	✦
complete a cloze activity								
write to support a particular point of view	✦	✦	✦	✦	✦	✦	✦	✦

Prim-Ed Publishing   www.prim-ed.com

Think and Save Ink

Mobile phone users can use the Short Message Service (SMS) to communicate with people. This service allows users to send a text (written) message to the person they wish to contact. Many people make up their own abbreviated message codes.

CODE EXAMPLES		
CUL8R = See you later	:-)BDAY = Happy Birthday	GR8 = Great
THAT'S:-(= That's sad	B2U = Back to you	THX = Thanks
XLNT = Excellent	BCNU = Be seeing you	ATB = All the best

1. Mr Fuller is a teacher who likes to make the pupils in his class think. He has found a good way to make them think and save himself some ink at the same time.

   Instead of writing comments in full on their schoolwork, he just writes the first letters of words. Can you work out what he may have meant when he wrote these comments?

   (a) For Jonathon, who scored one hundred per cent in a mathematics test.

   E W J. _____

   O H P ! _____

   K I U. _____

   (b) For Chad, who always tries hard.

   G W C. _____

   K T H. _____

   (c) For Nancy, whose book was beautifully neat and who often shows her work to Ms Gumber, the headteacher.

   V N W N. _____

   S Y BT M G. _____

   _____

   (d) For Patrick, whose work is often disappointing because he is quite clever but rather lazy.

   D E P. _____

   Y C D M B. _____

   _____

   (e) For Joshua, whose work is so messy that it needs to be done again.

   M W J. _____

   D T A N. _____

2. Your turn!

   Make up your own SMS codes:

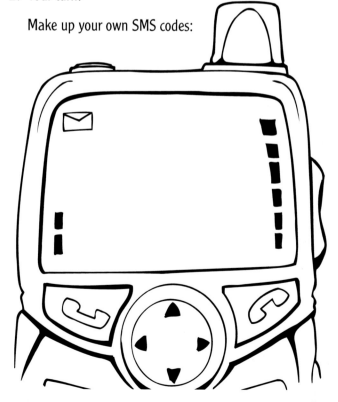

Prim-Ed Publishing   www.prim-ed.com

Why Did He Get the Sack?

Matthew Carter was very excited. It was Monday afternoon and he was setting off for the first taste of his new job as a nightwatchman at Noodlemeyer's Diamond and Jewellery Superstore.

His job was to guard the expensive jewellery in Noodlemeyer's huge safe.

That night he had a terrible dream. He dreamt that safecrackers were digging a tunnel under the building. In his dream they used state of the art cutting equipment to enter through the floor and clean the safe out completely.

Matthew thought nothing of it but the next night he had the same dream. It was so graphic that he woke up in a lather of sweat.

He went home and discussed the dreams he had had on successive nights with his wife. She said that it was probably just a coincidence brought on by the excitement of having his new nightwatchman's job in such a prestigious store.

When, however, he had the same dream on the third night he thought that it must have been a warning. Once before he had had a dream that had come true. Surely this dream repeating itself three times on consecutive nights

was warning him that the Superstore was the target of thieves. He felt certain that when he told Mr Noodlemeyer he would increase security so that the jewellery would be safe.

He waited back from work for Mr Noodlemeyer to arrive in the morning and told him how he had experienced the same dream on three consecutive nights. He suggested an increase in security to guard against the threat.

Matthew thought that Mr Noodlemeyer would be thankful for the warning but was greatly surprised when he sacked him on the spot. ◉

You, the comprehension detective, must find out why Mr Noodlemeyer sacked Matthew.

---

1. Use a dictionary to match each word with its meaning.

    (a) coincidence   •   •   illustrious

    (b) terrible   •   •   successive

    (c) huge   •   •   chance

    (d) prestigious   •   •   amazed

    (e) thankful   •   •   dreadful

    (f) consecutive   •   •   colossal

    (g) surprised   •   •   recommended

    (h) suggested   •   •   appreciative

Prim-Ed Publishing   www.prim-ed.com

2. Write short answers to the questions below.

(a) Why was Matthew Carter excited?

_____

_____

(b) What does a nightwatchman do?

_____

_____

(c) At which store did Matthew Carter work?

_____

_____

(d) What did he have to guard?

_____

_____

(e) What did Matthew dream?

_____

_____

(f) How did he feel about the dream at first?

_____

(g) What happened the next night?

_____

_____

(h) With whom did he discuss his dream?

_____

_____

(i) What happened once before when he'd had a dream?

_____

_____

(j) What did Matthew think Mr Noodlemeyer might do to ensure his jewellery was safe?

_____

_____

(k) When did Matthew tell Mr Noodlemeyer about his dream?

_____

_____

(l) How did Matthew think Mr Noodlemeyer would feel for telling him about his dream?

_____

_____

What do you think?

3. Find words with these meanings in the story.

(a) giving a vivid, lifelike picture _____

(b) following one after another _____

(c) highly regarded _____

(d) a chance happening linked to another recent happening _____

4. Being a clever comprehension detective you have probably worked out why Mr Noodlemeyer sacked Matthew.

Write the reason in a few sentences. _____

_____

_____

Prim-Ed Publishing   www.prim-ed.com

It's All in My Book!

Jonathon Millington was the toast of the country. In fact, he was the toast of many countries.

The clever young scientist had been the sole astronaut on the second manned space flight to the moon. The Australian had been chosen from a host of well-qualified candidates for the job. He would be alone on this, the second moon landing by a human.

There had been no hiccups at all in the flight until the landing itself, when the television satellite link broke down. No television pictures of the landing and moonwalk were seen on Earth. There was a story doing the rounds that some technicians believed someone or something had deliberately tampered with the television equipment. But these rumours soon fizzled out in the triumph of Millington's return.

Life was looking rosy for young Mr Millington. He was living in a perfume cloud with a number of beautiful starlets chasing him. His handsome face seemed to beam out at the world from every magazine stand. Film executives were falling over themselves with blank cheque offers of starring roles and a publisher had given him a huge advance for his soon to be released book about the landing.

Pursued by reporters, he dropped a bombshell that was to shatter current scientific thinking.

'Yes,' he said, 'believe it or not, there is life on the moon. I don't know what feeds it. I don't know how it survives in an environment with no atmosphere like the moon's. But I do know what I saw and heard. I'll never forget it . . . the bloodcurdling shriek that it makes. A scream like nothing you or I or anyone else, for that matter, have ever heard.

'Anyway guys, thank you. It's all going to be in my book. You can read about it there,' he said. 'Available at all good bookstores,' he added jokingly. He was soon whisked away to yet another society function in a gold limousine.

Sitting at home and watching proceedings on television was the well-respected scientist, Bunsen Von Braun. 'Ach du lieber! Dass silly boy isst einen dimvit. Vy do he telling ze lies for? He's going to be losing everysink because he iss telling zem dumkopf lies!' ◉

You, the comprehension detective, must do a little research to find out how Professor Von Braun knew that Millington was telling a sensational but untrue story to boost his book's sales.

---

1. What do you think is meant by the colloquial expression 'blank cheque offers'?

_____

_____

_____

2. In the passage it says of Millington, 'he was living in a perfume cloud'. What do you think this means?

_____

_____

_____

Prim-Ed Publishing   www.prim-ed.com

3. Write short answers to the questions below.

(a) Why was Jonathon Millington the toast of many countries? _____

_____

(b) From which country was Millington? _____

(c) What broke down just as his craft was landing? _____

(d) What did some technicians think? _____

(e) List three good things that happened to Millington after his return to Earth.

_____

_____

_____

(f) What 'bombshell' did Millington drop? _____

(g) What did Millington say the 'moon being' ate? _____

(h) What sort of noise did he say it made?   (i) What car was Millington travelling in?

_____   _____

(j) What did Professor Von Braun think of Millington's story? _____

_____

4. Choose the correct words from the word bank to complete the passage.

pitch	motion	travels	vibrates	cannot
plucked	vacuum	particles	higher	

When a tight string is _____ it _____, compressing the air particles nearby. These

_____ move in a wave _____. Sound _____ by means of these waves of

vibrating air particles. The faster things vibrate, the _____ the _____ of the sound they

make. Sound _____ travel in a _____ because there are no particles to vibrate.

5. If you know a little bit of elementary science, you should be able to tell why Professor Von Braun was suspicious of Millington's story.

_____

_____

_____

_____

Prim-Ed Publishing   www.prim-ed.com

The Great Train (Robbery) Mess Up

Detective Inspector Orth of the New York police department was stumped. There had been a robbery and the thief had escaped with over a million dollars worth of old, used banknotes.

The notes were on the way to a furnace where they were to be burnt because they were too worn to be kept in circulation. But the thief believed they should be kept in circulation a little while longer; at least until he got to use them.

The Detective Inspector had interviewed railway staff present at the scene and confided to his workmate and friend, Damien Garlick, that he thought the robbery had gone too smoothly. He thought that it must have been an inside job.

He had spoken to the ticket inspector and the driver of the electric train. Both claimed that they did not even know that a robbery had occurred until the guard crawled to the front carriage with blood trickling from a blow to the side of his face.

'There's something about the guard's story that doesn't seem right,' said Detective Inspector Orth. 'I think I'd better talk to him again.'

'It's just like I told you before,' said the guard, a shifty character by the name of Nicholas Todd. 'It all happened so quick. The whole thing was over before I knew it even started.

'There I was, minding my own business and the old banknotes, when some character grabs me from behind. Real strong he was too. Next thing I feel somethink like the train hit me and I see stars and little birds flyin' around.

'He works quick. I gets up an' sees him on the back of my van. But I didn't see nothin' of his face because of the smoke from the engine that's still floatin' around.

'You see, we'd just come out of a tunnel. Next thing he jumps—gone! And he's away with a cool million or so. Not bad for a few minutes work eh?'

'Very good, indeed,' said Detective Garlick nodding his head.

He and the Detective Inspector left the interview room.

'Got him,' said Detective Inspector Orth. 'He's part of this heist. A pity that he went to so much trouble to make up such a complicated story. It's what's going to put him in jail.' 👁

You, the comprehension detective, must find out what made Detective Inspector Orth so certain that Todd's story was untrue.

---

1. Write the dictionary meaning of the word 'heist'.

_____

_____

_____

2. Write short answers to the questions below.

(a) What had been stolen? _____

(b) To where were the notes being taken? _____

(c) Why were they being taken there? _____

(d) What is meant by an 'inside job'? _____

(e) What sort of train was it? _____

(f) When did the ticket inspector and driver first become aware of the robbery? _____

_____

(g) Where did Todd say that he caught a glimpse of the thief? _____

(h) Why did he say he was unable to see the thief's face? _____

(i) Why did he claim that the smoke was 'still floatin' around'? _____

(j) List the main characters in this story. _____

_____

3. Can you find the names of these famous trains in the puzzle?

Canadian Pacific
Stephenson's Rocket
Indian Pacific
Spirit of Progress
Southern Aurora
Shinkansen
Flying Scotsman

N	A	C	I	R	I	P	S	D	N
A	D	I	T	N	S	C	O	I	I
P	N	A	O	A	E	S	T	A	T
A	C	I	F	K	N	G	S	N	E
C	I	F	P	N	N	N	M	P	K
R	G	O	R	I	F	I	A	A	C
E	S	O	U	H	L	Y	N	C	O
S	E	H	T	S	A	R	C	I	R
S	R	N	A	U	R	O	I	F	S
S	T	E	P	H	E	N	S	O	N

4. Now that you have gathered lots of information about the crime, you, like the Detective Inspector, should know why Todd's story is untrue.

_____

_____

_____

_____

_____

7

Prim-Ed Publishing   www.prim-ed.com

The Rich Man's Lawns

Policewoman Corrine Lavis looked in wonder at the closely cut lawns of 'Plush Hectares', the country retreat of wealthy businessman, Rinaldo Voysey.

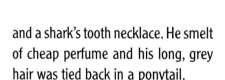

The front lawn was about the size of five football grounds and the grass was like a beautiful green carpet after two days of steady, soaking rain.

'Boy, would I like to live in a place like this!' thought the policewoman. She had come to investigate complaints from Voysey about the racehorse trainer, Natasha Payne.

There was bad blood between Ms Payne and Voysey. She had trained for him but refused to cooperate when he asked her not to play it square with a few of his horses. Voysey was as ruthless in his play as he was in business. When she didn't go along with him he'd sacked her. This made life hard for her. She'd borrowed plenty of money to move her training establishment closer to Plush Hectares and to upgrade it so it could accommodate over a hundred horses. Then he'd pulled the rug from under her by transferring his team of seventy horses to another trainer.

At last, Policewoman Lavis reached the huge oak doors. She was ushered inside and introduced to Voysey.

He sat in a big leather chair but looked gaudy rather than wealthy. He was a man of about fifty who liked to advertise his wealth. Each of his short, stubby fingers had a ring on it. The top four buttons of his shirt were undone, revealing a soft, pink chest and a shark's tooth necklace. He smelt of cheap perfume and his long, grey hair was tied back in a ponytail.

'Well, sir, you certainly have a lovely place here. Those beautiful, smooth lawns must cost a fortune to maintain. They look like a giant billiard table.'

'It's about dem dat I wanna talk to you about,' he croaked from the corner of his mouth. He was not a learned man. But when you run the markets in a big city like Harleyville people get to understand what you mean, even if it isn't out of some grammar textbook.

'Hey, how come dey sent a girl? Okay, I unnerstand. Equal rights and all that stuff. It's about dat creep, Payne. She's never forgiven me for giving her the flick. Ha! She couldn't train a monkey to eat bananas! Anyway, she keeps galloping dem slow nags she trains across my lawns. I ain't done nuttin' yet but she's askin' fer trouble, she is.'

'When did she do this?' asked the young policewoman.

'Since I made one of me best decisions and gave her marching orders as my trainer. Why the last time she done it was just an hour ago.'

Policewoman Lavis looked at Voysey's lawns.

'I think you must be stretching the truth a bit, Mr Voysey,' she said. 'In fact, I wouldn't be surprised if this whole story isn't just a petty way of getting revenge on Ms Payne.' 👁

You, the comprehension detective, must find out why Policewoman Lavis did not believe Voysey's story.

– Agistment Available –
Ample grazing on Plush Hectares
0379 666 900

8

1. Write short answers to the questions below.

    (a) What was the name of Rinaldo Voysey's country retreat? _____

    (b) How big was the front lawn? _____

    (c) What did the grass look like? _____

    (d) What had the weather been like? _____

    (e) What was Natasha Payne's job? _____

    (f) Voysey asked Natasha 'not to play it square' with some of his racehorses. What do you think this means?

    _____

    (g) Why had Natasha Payne borrowed a lot of money? _____

    _____

    (h) How did Voysey get back at Natasha Payne when she didn't go along with his plans?

    _____

    (i) What hung around Voysey's neck? _____

    (j) Describe Voysey's hair. _____

    (k) What business was Voysey in? _____

    (l) What did Voysey say about Natasha Payne's ability as a racehorse trainer?

    _____

    (m) What did Voysey claim Payne had been doing to get back at him?

    _____

    (n) When was the most recent time that she had supposedly done this?

    _____

2. (a) Voysey is described as appearing 'gaudy'.
        Write the dictionary definition of this word.

    _____

    _____

    (b) Voysey is described as not being 'learned'.
        Write the dictionary definition of this word.

    _____

    _____

3. In a few sentences tell why Policewoman Lavis did
    not believe Voysey's story. Answer in one or more
    sentences.

    _____

    _____

    _____

    _____

    _____

The Great Escape

Prim-Ed Publishing   www.prim-ed.com

Phyllis was prone to telling stories that some people thought were untrue. Whenever someone told her of some things they had done, Phyllis would say she had done them herself, known someone else who had done them or was related to someone who used to do them.

Her friend, Narelle, told her how she had stumbled from the last step climbing down a ladder after cleaning some leaves from her gutters. Phyllis immediately began to relate her adventures abseiling down sheer cliff faces in the Himalayas.

Another close friend, Robyn, told Phyllis how she had given some advice to her daughter and son-in-law who were having marriage problems. Phyllis took over the conversation, telling how a letter she had written to the United Nations was the cornerstone of peace negotiations in a major world trouble spot.

Worst of all, she always spoke in a loud voice so that people other than those she was directly talking to could hear.

When a person makes the sorts of claims that Phyllis did, people often disbelieve them even when they are telling the truth.

This was the case with the last piece of news she told the girls. They didn't believe her but her story was true in every detail.

It had to do with the fire that destroyed the fifty storey Umpire State Building, which was the new home of the De Vorzon Superstore.

'You could spend a month looking at all the shops,' said Phyllis. 'People on the ground look like dust mites from the top floor window. I was there on the day of the fire. When I heard that fire alarm I didn't think twice. I ran straight to the nearest window and jumped out.'

Narelle and Robyn looked at each other.

'You don't seem to have suffered any injuries,' said Narelle rather icily.

'Of course not!' snapped Phyllis, indignant at Narelle's apparent disbelief at her story.

Phyllis's story was true in every detail. Can you, the comprehension detective, fill in the details of her escape and explain what occurred?

---

1. Humans have built impressive buildings and monuments throughout history. Follow the clues to find the name of this very tall modern-day building. See if you can find in which city it is located.

    1 and 5 are in 'case' but not in 'cafe',

    3 is in 'rag' but not in 'rug',

    6 is in 'tummy' but not in 'dummy',

    8 is in 'cow' but not in 'cot'.

    2 and 9 are in 'eat' but not in 'cat',

    4 and 10 are in 'car' but not in 'cab',

    7 is in 'foil' but not in 'fail',

    ___ ___ ___ ___ ___   ___ ___ ___ ___ ___
     1   2   3   4   5   6   7   8   9   10

Prim-Ed Publishing   www.prim-ed.com

2.   Write short answers to the questions below.

(a)   What was Phyllis prone to doing?

_____

_____

(b)   List three ways that Phyllis would react if someone told her of things they had done.

•   _____

_____

•   _____

_____

•   _____

_____

(c)   What did Phyllis talk about when she heard that Narelle had stumbled from the ladder?

_____

_____

(d)   What did she talk about when Robyn mentioned her daughter's marriage problems?

_____

_____

(e)   What often happens to people who make extravagant claims?

_____

(f)   How did Phyllis speak when telling of her adventures?_____

_____

(g)   In which building was this adventure?

_____

(h)   Where had Phyllis been shopping?

_____

(i)   What was the lowest floor she could have been on?

_____

(j)   What was the highest floor Phyllis could have been on? _____

(k)   Does Phyllis say which floor she was on when the fire occurred? _____

(l)   What did Phyllis say people looked like from the top floor? _____

(m)   What injuries had Phyllis suffered as a result of her ordeal? _____

(n)   How did she escape from the fire?

_____

3.   Explain how Phyllis's story could be true.

_____

_____

_____

4.   Use a dictionary to write a meaning for each word below.

(a) negotiation _____

(b) indignant _____

Prim-Ed Publishing   www.prim-ed.com

The Insurance Claim

Things were grim in New York City. The 'Big Apple', as the locals called their hometown, was in the grip of the coldest winter in over a century. For five days the temperature had been at twenty degrees below zero.

Luckily there had been little snowfall so it was still possible to get around town. But people only ventured onto the streets when absolutely necessary. At the offices of We Never Pay Insurance Company there were other problems.

'I know this claim is a fraud,' said insurance claims manager, Loren Johnson. 'I just don't know how I can prove it. It's from a guy called Jared Butler. He's caught us out a few times before. It seems every time he insures something, it goes missing within a few months and we have to fork out the cash. This time it's a piece of jewellery—a watch. He said he lost it yesterday and he has a witness. It's going to set us back plenty this time unless I can prove his claim is a set up.'

'How much is 'plenty'?' asked her friend, unemployed television weather reporter, James Brault.

'About $20 000,' answered Loren.

'Wow! Show me the claim form,' said James.

He read it in a low voice. '"I was walking down to Elmo's Supermarket to buy some groceries. My friend, Stacey Pickett, was with me. We took a short cut across the park nearby. I had taken off my watch to adjust the time. It's a Rolloff – worth $20 000. I bought it after a winning day at the races. Just as I was adjusting it, I stumbled, fell and dropped the watch into the duck pond in the park. It quickly sank into the mud at the bottom of the pond. Stacey and I did our best to find it but it just seemed to vanish."

'He's a fake all right,' said James, 'and I don't think you'll have much trouble proving his story to be a lie.' ◉

You, the comprehension detective, must find out how James knew that Butler's story was untrue.

---

1. Unjumble the names of these timepieces then label them correctly.

itswartchw   inaslud   suagslhor

(a) _____   (b) _____   (c) _____

Prim-Ed Publishing   www.prim-ed.com

2. Write short answers to the questions below.

(a) Where is the story set?

_____

(b) What do the locals call their city?

_____

(c) What had the weather been like for the past five days?

_____

(d) Which insurance company did Loren Johnson work for?

_____

(e) What seemed to happen every time Butler insured something?

_____

(f) What had he lost in this story?

_____

(g) Who is James Brault?

_____

(h) What was the value of Butler's watch?

_____

(i) Where did Butler claim he was going?

_____

(j) Who was Butler's witness?

_____

(k) What brand was the watch?

_____

(l) Where did Butler claim he got the money to pay for the watch?

_____

(m) Where did Butler claim he dropped the watch?

_____

(n) Why did he say he couldn't find it there?

_____

Catch him out!

3. Match the temperatures below to their descriptions.

100°C   •   • the temperature on a cold winter's day

37°C   •   • a healthy body temperature

28°C   •   • the boiling point of water

3°C   •   • the freezing point of water

0°C   •   • the temperature on a hot summer's day

4. In a few sentences tell why James knew that Butler's story was not true.

_____

_____

_____

_____

Prim-Ed Publishing   www.prim-ed.com

Charming Beauregarde

Beauregarde Fitzwalters had a stylish name, but that was the only thing about him that was stylish. He was ill-mannered and oafish. A lazy, self-centred boy, he was a worry to his parents and a nuisance to the community.

If he wanted something, he wouldn't set his sights on working hard to save the money needed to buy it. Beauregarde would try to steal it. He would often be seen wearing his trademark baseball cap, tracksuit and trainers around the shopping centres of Sharp City.

When old Mrs Plum left her handbag unattended for just a brief moment in Lloyd's Megastore one afternoon, Beauregarde couldn't resist rummaging inside it and pulling out her purse. This done, he quickly placed it under his baseball cap. Even if he was stopped and searched, no-one would ever think of looking there. He'd been frisked once before and all the searchers found in his pockets was a packet of gum that he'd lifted earlier in the day. Beauregarde managed to take home a wealthy businessman's wallet that day.

When she came to the checkout, Mrs Plum soon found out that her purse was missing. The store security guard was called.

'Did you notice anyone near you acting suspiciously?' he asked.

'I did catch a glimpse of a young fellow wearing a cap. He seemed to hurry away oddly when I returned to my shopping trolley from the aisle I went into. I only wanted to put back a tin of cat food as I'm short of money this week. Unfortunately I caught just a glimpse of him and I can't really tell you what he looked like or what else he was wearing. I just remember the cap.'

Off duty policeman, Graeme Jenkinson, noticed the fuss and soon became involved. He suggested closing the store and asked Mrs Plum if she may be able to identify the culprit in a line-up. Several young men wearing caps agreed to participate in the line-up.

Rather than be seen to be acting suspiciously, Beauregarde agreed to participate. After all, he'd had on a pair of sunglasses from the display rack at the time. They hadn't appealed to him so he replaced them after deliberately bending the frames out of shape. And besides, he'd be so nice, so charming, that she'd think such a 'nice boy' wouldn't be capable of doing such a mean-spirited thing.

'Good afternoon,' said Beauregarde with a warm, sympathetic smile. To further display his manners he lifted his cap to her. 'I heard what happened. It's just dreadful.'

Poor Mrs Plum was unable to recognise any of the young men as the culprit.

'I'm sorry, I didn't get a good enough look at him. Besides these boys are all much too nice to have done such an awful thing anyway,' she said.

'Except one,' said Officer Jenkinson, walking over to Beauregarde and arresting him. 👁

Can you, the comprehension detective, tell how Officer Jenkinson knew that Beauregarde was the thief?

Prim-Ed Publishing   www.prim-ed.com

1. Use a dictionary to write the meaning of the word 'frisk'. There are a number of meanings.
    Choose the one meant in the story.

    _____

    _____

2. Write short answers to the questions below.

    (a) List four words that describe Beauregarde.

    _____   _____

    _____   _____

    (b) What wouldn't Beauregarde do to get something he wanted?

    _____

    (c) What would he try to do instead? _____

    (d) Describe how Beauregarde was usually dressed.

    _____   (e) Where had Mrs Plum left her handbag?

    _____   _____

    (f) What did Beauregarde steal from her?   (g) Where did he hide the stolen item?

    _____   _____

    (h) What did Officer Jenkinson suggest?_____

    (i) Why did Beauregarde agree to join the line-up? _____

    _____

    (j) Why did Beauregarde act in such an uncharacteristically pleasant manner? _____

    _____

    (k) What did Beauregarde do as a mark of respect   (l) Why was Mrs Plum unable to say who the probable
         when he spoke to Mrs Plum in the line-up?   thief was?

    _____   _____

3. Now that you've asked and answered the important questions and gathered vital evidence, you should know why
    Officer Jenkinson arrested charming Beauregarde.

    _____

    _____

    _____

    _____

Prim-Ed Publishing   www.prim-ed.com

Where's the Heir?

1. Before you read the story, use the dictionary to find the meaning of 'intestate'. Write the definition here.

_____

_____

_____

_____

The hunt was on for the heir to the fortune of the fabulously wealthy Scottish miser, Angus MacGurgle. MacGurgle so little liked the idea of parting with his money that he died intestate.

Had he made a will, he would probably have willed his money to himself. He had no known relatives. Now it was the job of special investigators to scour Scotland, and then the rest of the world if necessary, to find the person who was to inherit his enormous wealth.

The search extended to many countries, the last of them being Australia. The investigators were very thorough. Almost all of the 'Macs' in the phone books throughout the country were contacted but none, so far, had been the person they were looking for. At last there were just three people to be traced.

Iris MacWhirter finally returned from a trip to the 'old country' but a check of her details showed that she wasn't the person they were seeking.

Gupta MacDivot, too, was finally traced but he also wasn't the heir to the MacGurgle millions.

The only 'Mac' left untraced was a 'MacHinery' whose number hadn't answered for a month. The investigators decided to give it one last try and, to their surprise, there was a voice on the other end of the line.

'Sorry, mate,' said a male voice, 'no MacHinery lives here. This is a business number anyway—Fleegle's Machine Factory. We make all sorts of motors and machines here but we've been closed over the last month for the Christmas break. We've had this phone number for over fifteen years. I don't know how it got into the book under the name of MacHinery, though.'

So the investigators returned to Scotland with one big query. They had tracked down every Australian 'Mac' except 'MacHinery'. This was the one person in the whole world who could possibly be the heir to MacGurgle's millions but where was he? Did he even exist? Why was his number listed under Fleegle's Machine Factory? 👁

You, the Comprehension Detective, may be able to unravel the mystery of the missing MacHinery.

Prim-Ed Publishing   www.prim-ed.com

2. Write the dictionary meaning of 'heir'. (This word is pronounced 'air'.)

_____

_____

_____

3. Write short answers to the questions below.

    (a) Write the dictionary definition of 'miser'. _____

    (b) What did the investigator have to find? _____

    (c) Where did the investigators look first of all? _____

    (d) Which was the country they investigated last? _____

    (e) Which name beginning were they interested in? _____

    (f) Where had Iris MacWhirter been? _____

    (g) Who was the next person eliminated from the search? _____

    (h) Who was the last person the investigators wanted to contact? _____

    (i) Which business had MacHinery's phone number?   (j)   What was made there?

    _____   _____

    (k) Why hadn't anyone answered the phone there in the previous month? _____

    (l) Even though great care is always taken when books are typeset for publishing, sometimes mistakes still occur. Write the names of the three Australian people in the story in lower case (small) letters.

    _____   _____   _____

4. Explain what may have happened and why there probably wasn't any such person as MacHinery.

    _____

    _____

5. Match these accidental 'Mac' names with who they really are.   6. Write the words as they should be.

MacAroni •	• an Irish term of endearment (like 'darling')	_____
MacAroon •	• the art of tying decorative knots	_____
MacKerel •	• the universe	_____
MacRocarpa •	• a tree with lemon-scented leaves	_____
MacRocosm •	• a type of fish	_____
MacUshla •	• a light, sweet biscuit	_____
MacRame •	• a type of pasta	_____

Prim-Ed Publishing   www.prim-ed.com

Nuisance Call

Police Constable Stanley Webber was called into his chief's office.

'Another call-out for that woman, Meg Burrows. Claims there was a prowler in her garden last night,' said the chief.

'Oh no, not that woman again!' said PC Webber.

'It'll be a hoax call to get me out there, I bet you. I gave her a ride home in the patrol car after she fainted in the supermarket about six months ago. She hasn't left me alone since. She's got a crush on me. I changed my phone number last week because she kept ringing me up. No doubt this is her new way of getting my attention.'

PC Cox, Webber's partner, chimed in, 'Don't know what's up with him, Sir. She's a doll as far as I'm concerned.'

'Well I can't afford to have her wasting my officers' time on nuisance calls!' thundered the chief angrily. 'And you, Cox, had better concentrate on the job you're paid to do. Now listen, both of you. If you catch her out, then

throw the book at her. That'll make her think twice before she makes another nuisance call!'

PC Webber called into Ms Burrows's place to get her story.

'It happened about nine o'clock last night,' she began. 'I'd just come home from the cinema. As my car approached the house I saw a shadowy figure moving among the bushes in my front garden.'

'What did you do?' asked the handsome young officer.

'I was terrified. I stayed in the car all night. I turned off the motor but was too scared to turn off the headlights. I left them on all night. I must've dozed off at about four in the morning. When I woke up it was about nine in the morning.

'All the traffic going to work must have woken me. I started up my car straight away and drove it into my garage and then rang you. May I offer you a cup of tea?'

'No, thank you,' said PC Webber, 'I think you've taken up enough of my time today with that untrue story you've just told me.

'And let me warn you that if you ring the station with another nuisance call like today's I'll have to charge you with causing a public mischief.' 👁

> You, the comprehension detective, must find out why PC Webber didn't believe Ms Burrows's account of what happened to her.

---

1. Find the dictionary meaning of 'hoax'.

_____

_____

2. Write short answers to the questions below.

Prim-Ed Publishing   www.prim-ed.com

(a) List the four main characters in this story:

_____

_____

_____

_____

(b) Who is the imaginary character?

_____

(c) What had Meg Burrows claimed? _____

_____

_____

(d) What sort of call did PC Webber say it probably

was? _____

(e) When and where had he first met Meg?

_____

_____

(f) What had happened to her on that occasion?

_____

(g) Why did PC Webber change his phone number?

_____

(h) How did PC Webber feel about Meg?

_____

(i) How did the chief feel about what Cox said?

_____

(j) What did the chief mean when he said, 'Throw the

book at her'? _____

_____

(k) Approximately what time was it when Meg saw the

alleged prowler? _____

(l) Why didn't she turn off her headlights? _____

_____

(m) How long did she leave on the lights after switching

off the motor? _____

3. Write the dictionary meaning of the word 'allegation'.

_____

_____

_____

_____

_____

4. Discuss why newspaper, radio and television reporters refer to someone the police catch and believe may be responsible for a crime as the 'alleged' criminal.

_____

_____

_____

_____

_____

_____

5. Tell why PC Webber knew that Meg Burrows's story was not true.

_____

_____

_____

_____

_____

_____

Prim-Ed Publishing   www.prim-ed.com

Innocent or Guilty?

Jeff Boardman sat in the dock of the courtroom with a miserable look on his face.

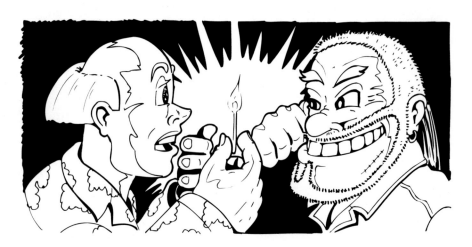

Despite protesting his innocence, he felt certain that he was about to be sentenced to a lengthy term for a burglary that he had not committed.

'But, Your Honour, I've been straight for 10 years now. I run a legitimate business,' he pleaded.

He looked at the stern faces of the judge and prosecutor and at the jury.

Sure, he'd had several convictions for petty theft and burglary in the past but they were all more than a decade ago. A stint in jail had taught him that crime did not pay.

It was the testimony of Noel Butling, a former partner in crime, that had proved most damaging. Jeff was sure that Butling had set up the burglary in his own flat to make a fraudulent insurance claim.

He recalled what Butling had said on the witness stand only a few hours earlier.

'It was about 2.00 a.m. on Tuesday morning, Your Honour. I heard a noise and tried to turn on the lamp by my bedside, but the criminal knew his stuff. He'd cut the power supply before attempting the caper. I fumbled around and found some safety matches on my chest of drawers. I couldn't find the box in the dark so I struck one on the wall. In the light of its flame I saw Boardman's face only twenty centimetres away from me. When you've spent three years in a cell with someone, you don't forget what he looks like. Anyway, the next thing I know it's morning and I wake up with a headache the size of Mount Everest and my flat's been cleaned out, including the expensive ring given to me by my fiancée, Kristine Hall. As you know, she's the heiress to the Hall chocolate fortune, so it's not a matter of money. It's the sentiment that came with it. I really love that dame.'

Jeff was brought back to the present by his lawyer leaning across and whispering to him.

'Don't worry, Jeff. This is a frame and I'm going to tell the jury that Butling is an unreliable witness right now,' she said.

Hall's Fine Chocolates

For the special person in your life
Hall of Fame
Special Occasions Box
found at all good chocolatiers

Hall of Fame
Special Occasions

You, the comprehension detective, must tell why Jeff's lawyer knew that Butling was not telling the truth.

1. Write the dictionary meaning of 'fraud'. _____

_____

2. Write the dictionary meaning of 'legitimate'. _____

_____

Prim-Ed Publishing   www.prim-ed.com

3. Write short answers to the questions below.

(a) Why was Jeff Boardman miserable?

_____

_____

(b) What had Boardman meant when he said he'd been

'straight' for ten years? _____

_____

(c) Which word describes the expression on the faces of

the judge and prosecutor? _____

(d) What had Boardman had convictions for in the past?

_____ and _____

(e) What reason did Boardman think Butling had for
setting up the burglary?

_____

_____

_____

(f) At what time did the supposed burglary occur?

_____

(g) Why didn't Butling's bedside lamp work?

_____

(h) What did Butling say he lit? _____

(i) Where did he strike this? _____

(j) Why did Butling say he knew Boardman's face so

well? _____

_____

(k) From whom had Butling received the ring?

_____

4. Sometimes technical knowledge is needed when
investigating crime. Find and then write the
dictionary definition of 'safety matches'.

_____

_____

_____

_____

_____

_____

5. Study your answers. Can you see where Butling went
wrong? In a few sentences, tell why Boardman's
lawyer knew that Butling wasn't telling the truth.

_____

_____

_____

_____

_____

_____

_____

6. What does the 'prosecutor' do in a court? Use a dictionary to find the definition of this word.

_____

_____

_____

Prim-Ed Publishing   www.prim-ed.com

The Jilted Lover

At last the rain had stopped. It had been raining nonstop for two weeks, pleasing farmers but annoying city folk.

Rain or no rain, private eye, Craig Mills, had been kept busy.

His current assignment was getting ugly. He had to warn off John McMahon, a would-be hardman, who had been pestering his former girlfriend, the showgirl, Brandy Power.

After a one-hour drive he came to McMahon's place—a small farm on the city outskirts.

The yard was a mess with building materials lying here and there in a disorderly state. McMahon was a do-it-yourself handyman type who seldom saw a job out to the finish. Half completed projects were all around; a partly finished workshed; an incomplete paling fence and a cement slab, probably for a carport but with no roof added yet. Mills stepped gingerly along the muddy pathway that led to McMahon's front door. Several times his foot sank to ankle depth in the soft mud, the result of fourteen days of uninterrupted rain. He rang the doorbell and was surprised when the door swung open only a matter of seconds later. McMahon stood before him, grubby and unshaven.

'Mr McMahon, my name is Craig Mills. I'm here for Brandy Power. She told me to let you know that if there are any unwelcome visits from you like the one two days ago, she will be contacting the police. No-one needs to put up with having someone they don't want around banging on their doors and windows for four hours.'

'Listen here, you . . . whoever you are. I don't know what you're talking about, see? Sure, I was sore at first about Brandy leaving me but I'm over it. I didn't go near her two days ago. I was right here all day pouring the concrete slab you see there for the carport I'm building. So, sorry, but bye-bye!' he said, slamming the door.

'Listen, I'm warning you for your own good,' said Mills, raising his voice to a shout that could be heard through the closed door. 'It's all over, okay? And if we're forced to involve the police, don't use that silly carport story again, will you?' 👁

You, the comprehension detective, must find out how Mills knew that McMahon's story was untrue.

---

1. Write the dictionary meaning of 'gingerly'.

Prim-Ed Publishing   www.prim-ed.com

2. Write short answers to these questions.

(a) For how long had it been raining? _____

(b) How had McMahon been pestering Brandy Power? _____

_____

(c) Where was McMahon's farm? _____

(d) What was the yard like? _____

_____

(e) List the three incomplete projects that are mentioned.

_____   _____

_____

(f) How do you know that the path was extremely muddy? _____

_____

(g) Describe McMahon's appearance when he opened the door. _____

_____

(h) What did McMahon claim he'd been doing two days before?

_____

(i) What would the weather have been like two days before? _____

3. Like a good detective, you have studied the facts. Answer in one or more sentences why Mills knew McMahon's story was untrue.

_____

_____

_____

4. Write the dictionary definition of 'harassment'.

_____

_____

_____

_____

5. The criminal usually has a motive. Write the dictionary definition of 'motive'.

_____

_____

_____

_____

Prim-Ed Publishing   www.prim-ed.com

Happy Holidays

'Aaah! This is the life!' said Detective Jake Young, reclining in a comfortable armchair and taking a sip of the cool drink his wife, Yoko, had made him.

After 18 months working without a break, they were both having a well-deserved holiday at Windies Resort on the Western Australian coast. The resort was near the pearling town of Broome, in the Kimberley, where the tides rise and fall dramatically—sometimes several metres.

The phone rang in the top cop's luxury suite, a sound he hoped he wouldn't hear for the rest of his stay. It was his boss, Chief Inspector Rex Derrick, phoning from Perth. 'Jake, sorry to ruin your holiday, but there's something I need you to check out for me. One of the locals, a bit of a no-good I'm told, by the name of Gavin Mitchell, claims he was roughed up and his shop burnt down by some thugs. This sort of thing's happened to him before—same setup. We were suspicious but couldn't prove anything.'

'Okay boss, I'll check it out and see if we can come up with a result. We'd probably only have to pay half of what we do in insurance premiums if we could stop this sort of stealing,' said the weary detective.

He turned to his wife. 'Darling, I've got to look into something for the boss. Can you take the kids to the cinema? 'The Wild Artichoke' is showing at the complex. They'll like that. I hope I can get this thing cleared up today so we can spend a bit of time together.'

Young met Mitchell, a miserable looking wretch, at the scene of the supposed crime, a burnt-out fast food place near the beachfront. It was low tide and the seabirds were making the most of it, feeding on the creatures temporarily exposed from their water covering.

'Tell me exactly what happened,' asked Young.

'I didn't get a good look at them but they meant to do me in, good and proper,' said Mitchell in his high-pitched voice.

He walked Young down to the water's edge on a deserted part of the beach.

'They knocked me out,' continued Mitchell, 'and chained me to this cement block you see here.'

He pointed to a cement block partly covered by water, the type used to anchor buoys.

'The chain was only about half a metre long. I came to again but then one of them slugged me hard and I was out cold for about fifteen hours. When I came to this time I managed to prise open the shackle on my foot with that old iron anchor piece you see there. I staggered the two kilometres to my shop to ring the police, only to see that they'd continued the dirty work there.

'Why did they have to burn it? It'll ruin me!'

'I think you've ruined yourself. Burning down your own shop for the insurance money means you'll get nothing. Oh, forgive me, you will get to have a nice rest for a while in jail. The story you've told me is a lie. Now, let's start over again, and tell me the truth this time.'

You, the comprehension detective, must now work out how Detective Young knew that Mitchell's story wasn't the truth.

Gavin's for Great Grub

This week's special: 'The Works' Crabburger – with large fries

4 Beach Road, Windies Resort

Prim-Ed Publishing   www.prim-ed.com

1. Write short answers to the questions below.

(a) What was the location of the resort?

_____

(b) Which town was it near? _____

(c) What did Jake's boss think Mitchell was really after?

_____

(d) What is unusual about the tides here?

_____

_____

(e) What were the seabirds doing?

_____

(f) What did Gavin Mitchell say had happened to him?

_____

_____

(g) How do fraudulent insurance claims affect people

who buy insurance policies? _____

_____

_____

(h) Where was the tide when Young met Mitchell?

_____

(i) To what did Mitchell claim he was chained?

_____

(j) How long was the chain?

_____

(k) For how long did he claim he was unconscious?

_____

(l) What did he say he used to prise open the shackle?

_____

(m) How far did he have to walk before telephoning

the police? _____

(n) What would Mitchell get when the insurance
company found out he'd burnt down his own

shop? _____

2. In a few sentences, explain why Mitchell's story
was untrue.

_____

_____

_____

_____

_____

_____

_____

_____

_____

_____

3. Find words with these meanings in the story.

(a) very noticeably _____

(b) spoil _____

(c) a thistle-like plant used as a vegetable

_____

(d) a group of buildings connected to each other

_____

(e) for a short time _____

(f) to lever something open _____

(g) not covered _____

Prim-Ed Publishing   www.prim-ed.com

The Kidnapped Kidnapper

The sun beat down relentlessly in a cloudless sky, as it had for the past week. But that wasn't the only reason for the cascading sweat that ran down Grover T. Alexander's worried face.

'Sure, he's a wastrel and a spendthrift, but he's still my son and I don't want him hurt.'

The multimillionaire oil baron was at police headquarters. He was renowned as a hard but fair man. His son, Gregor, was just the opposite and resented his father bringing him up the hard way. Daddy had made him start at the bottom in his business. He wanted someone worthy to take over the business when he passed on and hoped against hope that it would be his boy—the apple of his eye. How better to give him an understanding of the job than by making him come through the ranks on his own merits. This didn't suit Gregor. He wanted to have fun now! To Gregor, fun meant spending money— lots of money!

It seemed Gregor had been kidnapped. The kidnappers had sent a ransom note and, with it, was a lock of Gregor's hair. The note promised that if the money wasn't handed over within the next three days, Gregor would be seriously hurt.

Alexander Senior had followed the instructions to the letter but, so far, there had been no sign of Gregor and time was running out.

'We've got a hundred officers working on the case,' said Chief of Police, Todd 'Snapper' Harris. 'We'll find him.'

Suddenly, without a word of warning, the door burst open. Gregor stumbled in and collapsed on the floor.

He was a handsome young man but his clothes were dishevelled and grimy. No doubt, he'd endured some rough treatment at the hands of the kidnappers. He had tangled blond hair, blue eyes and very pale skin.

Grover T. Alexander ran to his son and embraced him. He was overcome with emotion.

'Dad! Am I glad to see you!' said Gregor. He seemed quite relaxed for someone who had been through a terrible ordeal.

Waiting for the right moment, Harris said, 'You'll have to tell us everything you can. These people have tasted success. If we don't catch them they'll definitely try again, and this time the victim may not be so lucky.'

'Well, they were very professional—I'll give them credit for that,' said young Alexander. 'I didn't see their faces at any time, but I think there were three of them.'

'They blindfolded me and took me out into the country somewhere. Then they took off my shirt and handcuffed me to some sort of iron stake or pole out in an open paddock.

'Then they gagged me so I couldn't shout and get anyone's attention. Anyway, it was so quiet out there —must have been in the middle of nowhere. I doubt there'd be anyone there to hear me, even if I did call out. At least they had the decency to give me a bit of food and some water every few hours. I needed it too, out in that sun all day.

'Well, then Dad came good with the money so they bundled me into the car and tossed me out in front of Police Headquarters. That's when I came in. Is there anything else you need to know?'

'No,' said Harris, 'you've told us enough already, but you'll need to know a good lawyer. We'll be laying charges against you for setting up this fake kidnapping so that you could get your hands on some of your father's money.' 👁

You, the comprehension detective, must try to find out how Harris knew that Gregor Alexander's story about the kidnapping was untrue.

Prim-Ed Publishing   www.prim-ed.com

1. Write short answers to the questions below.

    (a) What had the weather been like for the last week?

    _____

    (b) Which two words did Grover T. Alexander use to describe his son?

    _____   _____

    (c) What had made Alexander rich? _____

    (d) Why had Alexander made his son start at the bottom in his business? _____

    _____

    (e) Why didn't this suit Gregor? _____

    (f) What accompanied the ransom note? _____

    (g) How many days did Alexander have to pay the money? _____

    (h) What did the kidnappers say would happen to Gregor if the ransom was not paid? _____

    (i) How many officers were working on the case?

    _____

    (j) What colour was Gregor's hair?

    _____

    (k) What colour were Gregor's eyes?

    _____

    (l) What sort of skin did he have?

    _____

    (m) What was unusual about the way Gregor behaved when he turned up?

    _____

    (n) Why did Harris say it was most important to catch the kidnappers quickly?

    _____

    (o) Why couldn't Gregor describe the kidnappers?

    _____

    (p) To what did Gregor say he'd been handcuffed?

    _____

    (q) What was the location of the stake or pole?

    _____

    (r) How did the kidnappers ensure that Gregor could not call out for help? _____

    (s) What decent thing did Gregor say they had done?

    _____

    (t) Where had the kidnappers released Gregor?

    _____

2. Now that you have gathered the clues like a good detective, can you tell why Harris thought Gregor's story was not true? All the clues are important. Good detective work is not about isolated incidents but about the overall picture. Answer in a few sentences.

    _____

    _____

    _____

Prim-Ed Publishing   www.prim-ed.com

Sir Marvo the Dull

Sir Marvo the Dull, the World's Least Interesting Magician, had just begun his magic show.

'And now,' he announced in a booming voice, 'an amazing trick! I will throw this ball as hard as I can. It will leave my hand at tremendous speed, stop and come straight back to me. As you can see, there is no elastic or string attached to the ball and it will not strike anything and rebound to me.'

There was a drum roll. He paused, set himself . . . and threw!

The crowd did not gasp as they often do at magic shows. They groaned.

'That's not magic!' cried a voice in the crowd.

And yet the trick had worked exactly as Marvo had said it would.

'Oh, I see! A difficult audience! Not good enough for you, eh?' stormed Marvo. 'You will love this, my most amazing and bewildering trick. In my right hand I have a pistol, in my left hand a hat. I shall raise my pistol so that the barrel is pointing to the sky.

My assistant, the lovely Louise, will blindfold me, then take the hat from me and hang it up. I shall walk fifty paces, stop, turn and shoot a bullet straight through the hat.'

Sir Marvo did exactly what he said he would do but nobody in the audience was very impressed. How could he have done such a difficult sounding trick but still fail to get a single gasp from his audience?

'And that concludes the show for this evening!' said Sir Marvo.

The audience filed out of the huge theatre looking rather bewildered. Sir Marvo may be playing at a venue near you now. Check the newspapers. It is said he has some fascinating new tricks in his act now. ◉

> You, the comprehension detective, must solve the puzzle of Sir Marvo's tricks. Why did most people think they were dull?

---

1. See how many words of three letters or more you can make from 'magician'. No proper nouns. Ten is a good score.

Prim-Ed Publishing   www.prim-ed.com

2 . Write short answers to the questions below.

(a) What sort of magician is Sir Marvo described as being? _____

(b) What equipment did he use for his first trick?

_____

(c) What was he going to do with this object?

_____

(d) What unusual thing would it then do?

_____

(e) In which direction does a submarine travel to escape attack? _____

(f) In which direction does a hot air balloon travel when it leaves the ground? _____

(g) Study your answers to (e) and (f) because they will give you a clue about how Sir Marvo's trick worked. In which direction could Sir Marvo throw the ball to ensure that it came straight back to him?

_____

(h) Which two pieces of equipment were needed for his second trick?

_____

(i) What was in his left hand? _____

(j) What was in his right hand? _____

(k) Which three things would the lovely Louise do?

_____

_____

(l) How many paces would Sir Marvo take? _____

(m) What would he then do?

_____

_____

(n) Are we told where the lovely Louise hung the hat? | **yes** | **no** |

(o) Where may she have hung the hat in order to allow Sir Marvo to do the trick easily?

_____

3. Draw and colour a poster advertising Sir Marvo's next show.

4. Highlight the words associated with INTERESTING yellow and those associated with DULL red.

tiresome   ennui

fascinating   boring

tedious

exciting

painstaking   laborious

absorbing   engrossing

Prim-Ed Publishing   www.prim-ed.com

Inside Job

'We're at the crime scene now, Chief,' said policewoman Jessica Davies into the telephone's mouthpiece.

'Yes, that's right. Fitzpatrick's Jewellery Shop. Constable Roberts is interviewing Mr Fitzpatrick right now. He seems to think it was an 'inside job', carried out by someone who works here now or has worked here in the past. Okay, thanks Chief. I'll go and see what he's got to say. 'Bye now.'

Policewoman Davies went over to her partner, Constable Shaun Roberts, who was speaking to the owner, Albert Fitzpatrick.

'I got here early this morning as I always do,' said Fitzpatrick. 'When I opened the safe I could see straight away that the diamonds were missing. The thief, whoever he or she was, wasn't interested in anything else. The sapphires, rubies, emeralds and gold were all left alone.'

'I see,' said Constable Roberts. 'And you think the robbery was carried out by an insider—someone who works here. What makes you think that?'

'It's too neat. Nothing's been smashed or broken. The safe's been opened without explosives. I'll show you. It's in the room out the back. I'm certain someone's had duplicate keys made. Only my partner, Pete Moss, and myself have keys. We usually take it in turns opening the shop. Pete's on holiday at the moment so I've been getting things ready in the morning.'

'Does Mr Moss know about the robbery?' asked Constable Roberts.

'No, nobody does. As soon as I saw what had happened I rang you.'

Just then Wilbur Lawrence, an employee at the shop came in.

'Good morning, Mr Fitzpatrick. Say, what's going on? Why are the police here?' asked Lawrence.

'We've been robbed. I'll show you what was taken when the police have gone. This could ruin me,' said a worried Fitzpatrick.

'So, we're looking for a diamond thief. They put away Antony MacFarland, didn't they? His speciality was diamonds, wasn't it?' asked Lawrence.

'Yes, we got him and you might be sharing a cell with him soon,' said Policewoman Davies. 'I think you know quite a bit about this robbery, Mr Lawrence. Now, talk!' 👁

See if you can use your comprehension and detective skills as well as Policewoman Davies. Why did she think that Lawrence had something to do with the robbery?

---

1. Did you know that there are seven smaller words of two letters or more hiding in POLICEWOMAN. They are police, woman, man, an, ice, lice and *Oman (*a country in the Middle East).

   Now see if you can find seven smaller words hiding in INTERVIEWING.

   (a) ___ ___   (b) ___ ___ ___ ___   (c) ___ ___ ___ ___ ___   (d) ___ ___ ___ ___

   (e) *___ ___ ___ ___ ___   (f) ___ ___ ___ ___ ___ ___ ___

   (g) ___ ___ ___ ___ ___ ___ ___

   * Means 'to bury'.

Prim-Ed Publishing   www.prim-ed.com

2. Write short answers to the questions below.

  (a) Where was the crime committed? _____

  _____

  (b) Which two police officers attended the crime scene?

  _____

  _____

  (c) What is meant by an 'inside job'? _____

  _____

  (d) Which two men were partners in the jewellery shop?

  _____

  _____

  (e) What was stolen? _____

  (f) What was left behind? _____

  _____

  (g) Why did Mr Fitzpatrick think it was an inside job?

  _____

  _____

  (h) Who had keys to the shop? _____

  _____

  (i) Where was Pete Moss when the crime took place?

  _____

  (j) Apart from Fitzpatrick and the police, who knew about

  the robbery? _____

  (k) Which employee walked in? _____

  _____

  (l) What did Mr Fitzpatrick say he would show the

  employee when the police left? _____

  _____

  (m) What did Antony MacFarland specialise in stealing?

  _____

  (n) Why couldn't MacFarland be the thief? _____

  _____

3. Now that you have gathered the clues, can you tell why Policewoman Davies suspected that Lawrence was involved in the robbery? Good detective work is not about isolated incidents but about the overall picture.

  _____

  _____

  _____

  _____

  _____

  _____

  _____

  _____

4. Match the jewels with their descriptions. You may need to use a dictionary.

  amethyst   diamond   emerald
  sapphire   ruby

  (a) precious stone consisting of a violet or purple type of quartz

  _____

  (b) precious stone that varies in colour from red to pale rose

  _____

  (c) bright green precious stone

  _____

  (d) a transparent blue precious stone

  _____

  (e) clear colourless crystal form of pure carbon

  _____

Prim-Ed Publishing   www.prim-ed.com

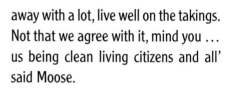

Crooks Never Prosper

'C'mon you mug,' said three time loser, 'Moose' Bullman. Bullman was the getaway driver in a planned robbery. Already, he'd been waiting in the hot sun of the open air carpark for close to half an hour. All that time, the motor had been running.

At last he saw the bank's doors burst open and his accomplice, 'Ferret' Ferguson, raced over to the waiting car. Ferguson, too, had a string of armed robberies to his name.

'What took you so long?' yelled Moose angrily.

'Damn front door. I tried to push it open but it wouldn't go,' answered Ferret.

'You mean the door with the 'Pull' sign on it?' asked Moose. 'I told you to be careful of that. That's how the police caught you last time.'

'Aw, just shut up and drive,' said Ferret.

Spinning the wheels in the carpark, Moose took off and was out of sight in no time.

Ferret put the cash-filled money bag on the back seat of the car.

Before the police arrived at the crime scene, Moose had made a clean getaway and had the car under cover in his lockup garage.

Laughing, giving each other 'high fives' and punching each other on the shoulder, the two crooks went inside. A mere minute later, two police officers knocked on Moose's front door. They'd come to return some car parts which they suspected Moose of stealing. Luckily for the two 'crims', the police were unable to prove their suspicions.

'Okay, coppers. Bring 'em in here,' said Moose, smirking as he led them into the garage.

'What a laugh!' thought the two criminals. A few minutes earlier they'd cleaned out the bank and now had two policemen returning stolen property to them. What made it a greater laugh still was that the money from the robbery was in the bag on the back seat, staring the two policemen in the face.

Policeman Dave Santini looked at Moose's beautifully polished car. Though he looked like a grub himself, Moose was devoted to that car. Santini went to place his hand on the car to feel the glossy paintwork but then pulled it away sharply.

'Nice motor,' said PC Victor Fox, Santini's partner. Then, looking at Moose, he asked, 'Been anywhere in it lately?'

'No, it's been in the garage all morning,' answered Ferret. 'Go ahead, touch it. You'll never own one on a copper's wage,' he added.

'Yeah, don't you coppers think of changing sides? After all, 'crims' get away with a lot, live well on the takings. Not that we agree with it, mind you ... us being clean living citizens and all' said Moose.

'Uh-huh,' said PC Fox, lifting an eyebrow. 'You say the car's been in the garage all morning, eh? Well I don't believe you.'

'Why would you be lying to us if you didn't have anything to hide? Mind if we have a closer look?' asked Constable Santini. 'Say, Moose, what's this on the back seat?' asked Santini, pointing to the cash-filled bag.

Moose and Ferret ran for it but were rounded up a few days later. Both are serving lengthy stretches inside for armed robbery. 👁

Something aroused PC Santini's suspicion and led to him asking for a 'closer look'. Use your comprehension and detective skills to find out what it was.

1. Write short answers to the questions below.

Prim-Ed Publishing   www.prim-ed.com

(a) What was 'Moose' Bullman's part in the bank robbery?

_____

(b) What sort of day was it? _____

(c) For how long had he been waiting in the car?

_____

(d) What was Ferguson's nickname? _____

(e) Why had Ferguson found it difficult to open the door?

_____

(f) Where did Ferguson put the cash-filled bag?

_____

(g) What did Bullman do with the car after the robbery?

_____

(h) What three things did Bullman and Ferguson do as they went inside the house?

_____

_____

_____

(i) How long after Bullman and Ferguson went inside did the police arrive? _____

(j) Why were the police there? _____

_____

(k) What description is given of Bullman's car?

_____

(l) What is Bullman described as looking like?

_____

(m) Why did Santini reach out to touch the car?

_____

(n) What did he do next? _____

_____

(o) Where did Bullman say the car had been all morning?

_____

(p) Why did Bullman suggest that the police change sides and become 'crims'? _____

_____

(q) Why did Santini ask for 'a closer look'? _____

_____

(r) Where are 'Moose' and 'Ferret' now? _____

_____

2. Why did PC Santini become suspicious of Moose and Ferret's story? Answer in a few sentences.

_____

_____

_____

_____

_____

_____

3. Write an AFFIRMATIVE and NEGATIVE statement for the proposition:

'Criminals are better served by the justice system than their victims.'

Perhaps your class could debate this topic.

Affirmative _____

_____

_____

Negative _____

_____

_____

Prim-Ed Publishing   www.prim-ed.com

Late Again

Jeremy Gilchrist's mother was pleased. At last the young man had a job. Admittedly it was not terribly well paid.

Jeremy worked as a bellhop at the plush Walford Gastoria Hotel. His duties involved showing visitors to their rooms, carrying their luggage and supplying food or drink for room service.

Jeremy looked splendid in his uniform. It comprised crisp, navy blue trousers, a smart, navy blue jacket with gold trimming and the choice of either navy blue or black socks.

Jeremy was quite good at his job but there was one thing that annoyed his boss, Mr Silverstein. Too often, Jeremy was late for work. Mr Silverstein had given him numerous warnings about this. Now, he was on his last chance.

'I'm sorry, my boy,' said Mr Silverstein, 'but when you're late it means we're short-staffed. Someone has to do your job as well as their own.'

The next morning, despite Mr Silverstein's warning, Jeremy arrived three-quarters of an hour late.

'Jeremy,' said Mr Silverstein. 'I told you yesterday that you'd run out of chances. I'm really pleased with your work at the hotel and don't want to lose you. Could it be that, just this once, you have a really good reason for being late?'

'Yes, really, Mr Silverstein. You won't believe my bad luck this morning. I was up and dressed in plenty of time but as I pulled out my drawer with socks in it, it became stuck. I could just fit two fingers in to pull out one sock at a time.

There were ten blue socks and ten black socks in the drawer. As luck would have it, I had to pull out eleven socks before I had a pair the same colour – the black ones I've got on now.

Well, this made me late for the bus, so I had to wait for the next one.'

'I'm sorry that you've lied to me Jeremy. Perhaps you should have listened harder at school. I'm afraid you'll have to look for a new place to work,' said Mr Silverstein. 👁

Use your detective and comprehension skills to find out how Mr Silverstein knew that Jeremy was telling a lie.

---

1. Match each word with its meaning.

    (a) premature •   • on time

    (b) tardy •   • late

    (c) punctual •   • early

What do you think?

Prim-Ed Publishing   www.prim-ed.com

2. Write short answers to the questions below.

(a) What was Jeremy Gilchrist's new job? _____

(b) Where did Jeremy work? _____

(c) List three duties that Jeremy's job involved.

- _____

- _____

- _____

(d) Describe Jeremy's work uniform. _____

_____

_____

(e) Who was Jeremy's boss? _____

(f) What annoyed his boss? _____

(g) How did this problem affect other members of staff? _____

(h) How late was Jeremy the next morning? _____

(i) What did Jeremy say happened when he pulled out his drawer with socks in it? _____

(j) How did he say he got the socks out? _____

(k) How many socks were in the drawer? _____

(l) How many of each colour did he have? _____

(m) How many did he say he pulled out before having a pair the same colour? _____

(n) What happened as a result? _____

3. In a few sentences, explain why Mr Silverstein knew that Jeremy was lying.

_____

_____

_____

_____

_____

_____

_____

_____

_____

4. Write the dictionary meanings of the words below. Both of them have something to do with large hotels like the Walford Gastoria.

(a) concierge _____

_____

_____

(b) dumb waiter _____

_____

_____

Prim-Ed Publishing   www.prim-ed.com

Bad Day for Bobby

'You think he torched the car himself for the insurance money?' asked Senior Sergeant Darren Martin.

'Yes, Sir, I do. But I don't know how we're going to prove it,' replied Police Constable Sam Payne. 'It's all too neat and tidy for my liking.'

They were talking about the theft and burning of businessman, Bobby Powell's car. It was a new model Mercedes and very expensive.

'Let's go over his statement again,' suggested the senior officer.

Constable Payne pulled out the filing cabinet drawer and located the statement that Powell had given the day after the supposed theft. He began reading it aloud.

'"Monday, January 22nd, 2006 … Statement given by Robert Gregory Powell… Yesterday I was going about my business as usual. I typed some letters on my word processor and answered my emails. I work from my office at home. At about 11 o'clock that morning I drove into town. I went into the post office to buy some stamps. After doing this I climbed into my car again and went to the bank. It was quite busy so I had to park around a corner about two streets away. When I had just about reached the bank I realised I'd left some papers I needed in the car. I went back and saw that my car was missing. I should have called the police straight away, I know, but I took my wife's car and went looking for the Mercedes.

'"I saw some smoke on a deserted road on the outskirts of town—near the city garbage dump. When I drove down there I saw the remains of my car, still smoking." End of statement.'

'Say, this bird's got a bit of form with us, hasn't he? asked Sergeant Martin.

'Yes, Sir,' replied Payne. 'Mostly small time scams. Last year he advertised a sure-fire method of cutting household bills in half.'

'Oh yes, I remember now. People sent him money and he mailed them a pair of scissors. We got him on a similar scam a year earlier.'

'Oh? What was that one, Sir?' asked Payne.

'He ran an ad promising to tell the secret used by wealthy people to become rich,' said the Senior Sergeant.

'And what did they get for their money, Sir?' enquired Payne.

'They got a single sheet of writing paper with the word 'CHEAT' written on it in bold letters.'

'Anything connected to insurance money before?' asked the young constable.

'Two things. His wife once, supposedly, had some jewels stolen. Powell's story was on the nose but, in the end, the insurance company had to pay out.

'The other time is now. But he won't get away with it this time. He's going to spend some time in jail, making number plates for other people's expensive cars,' said the Senior Sergeant, closing the drawer of the filing cabinet. 'Come on! Let's go and drag him in here now and charge him. The story he told in his statement has to be a lie.' 👁

Use your comprehension and detective skills to find out how the Senior Sergeant knew that Powell was not telling the truth in his statement.

1. Write short answers to the questions below.

Prim-Ed Publishing   www.prim-ed.com

(a) What sort of car did Powell have?_____

(b) What did Sam Payne think Powell had done to the

car? _____

(c) What did Senior Sergeant Martin suggest they go over

again? _____

(d) What was the day of Powell's statement?

_____

(e) On which day did the events take place?

_____

(f) What did Powell say he'd done before going into town?

_____

(g) Where did he go first? _____

(h) Where did he go next? _____

(i) How far from the bank did he have to park?

_____

(j) Why did he go back to the car? _____

_____

(k) What did he do rather than go to the police straight

away? _____

_____

(l) Where did he find his car? _____

_____

(m) What had Powell sent to people to help them cut

household bills in half? _____

(n) What did he advise people to do to become rich?

_____

(o) On what else had Powell claimed insurance?

_____

(p) What did Senior Sergeant Martin suggest Powell

would be making in jail? _____

_____

2. Senior Sergeant Martin quickly worked out that Powell was a fraud. He paid special attention to the clues. In a few sentences, tell where Powell went wrong.

_____

_____

_____

_____

_____

_____

_____

_____

You've got talent for this detective stuff!

3. List the names of five car makers.

_____

_____

_____

_____

_____

4. Draw and colour your 'dream' car.

Think and Save Ink......................Page 1
1. (There are other possibilities.)
   (a) Excellent work, Jonathon! One hundred percent! Keep it up.
   (b) Good work, Chad. Keep trying hard.
   (c) Very neat work, Nancy. Show your book to Ms Gumber.
   (d) Disappointing effort, Patrick. You can do much better.
   (e) Messy work, Joshua. Do this again neatly.
2. Teacher check

Why Did He Get the Sack? ... Pages 2 – 3
1. (a) chance   (b) dreadful
   (c) colossal   (d) illustrious
   (e) appreciative   (f) successive
   (g) amazed   (h) recommended
2. (a) he was starting a new job
   (b) guard a premises at night
   (c) Noodlemeyer's Diamond and Jewellery Superstore
   (d) the jewellery in the safe
   (e) safecrackers were digging a tunnel under the building to enter through the floor and clean out the safe
   (f) thought nothing of it
   (g) he had the same dream
   (h) his wife
   (i) it had come true   (j) increase security
   (k) after having the dream three times
   (l) thankful
3. (a) graphic   (b) consecutive
   (c) prestigious   (d) coincidence
4. If he was a nightwatchman he should not have been asleep and dreaming but awake and watching.

It's All in My Book! .... Pages 4 – 5
1. blank cheque – a cheque with the amount left for the payee to fill in
2. perfume cloud – very favourable circumstances
3. (a) He had been the sole astronaut on the second manned space flight to the moon.
   (b) Australia
   (c) television satellite link
   (d) someone or something had tampered with the equipment
   (e) pursued by beautiful starlets, face on magazine covers, film offers, book publishing offers
   (f) there is life on the moon
   (g) he did not know
   (h) bloodcurdling shriek
   (i) gold limousine
   (j) knew he was telling lies
4. plucked, vibrates, particles, motion, travels, higher, pitch, cannot, vacuum

5. Millington said that the moon had no atmosphere but that he heard a bloodcurdling shriek. Sound cannot travel where there is no atmosphere.

The Great Train Robbery (Mess Up) .... Pages 6 – 7
1. a heist is a robbery
2. (a) a million dollars worth of old banknotes
   (b) to a big furnace   (c) to be burnt
   (d) a crime committed by someone working on the premises where it occurred
   (e) electric train
   (f) when the guard came crawling to the front carriage
   (g) on the back of the van
   (h) smoke from the engine hid it
   (i) they had just come out of a tunnel
   (j) Detective Inspector Orth, Damien Garlick, Nicholas Todd
3.

N	A	C	I	R	I	P	S	D	N
A	D	I	T	N	S	C	O	I	I
P	N	A	O	A	E	S	T	A	T
A	C	I	F	K	N	G	S	N	E
C	I	F	P	N	N	N	M	P	K
R	G	O	R	I	F	I	A	A	C
E	S	O	U	H	L	Y	N	C	O
S	E	H	T	S	A	R	C	I	R
R	N	A	U	R	O	I	F	S	
S	T	E	P	H	E	N	S	O	N

4. It was an electric train so there would be no smoke in the tunnel.

The Rich Man's Lawns .... Pages 8 – 9
1. (a) Plush Hectares
   (b) about the size of five football fields
   (c) beautiful green carpet
   (d) two days of steady rain
   (e) racehorse trainer
   (f) to stop them from trying to win
   (g) to move her training establishment closer to Plush Hectares
   (h) sacked her; gave his seventy racehorses to another trainer
   (i) shark's tooth necklace
   (j) long, grey and tied back in a ponytail
   (k) ran the markets
   (l) couldn't train a monkey to eat bananas
   (m) galloping her horses across Voysey's lawns (trespass)
   (n) an hour earlier
2. (a) extravagantly bright or showy so as to be tasteless
   (b) educated
3. It had been raining. The lawns were soft. If Payne had galloped her horses over them the lawns would show evidence of this. They are described as being smooth like a giant billiard table.

The Great Escape .... Pages 10 – 11
1. Sears Tower (located in Chicago, USA)
2. (a) telling stories that people thought were untrue
   (b) done them herself, knew someone who had done them, be related to someone who used to do them
   (c) told how she abseiled down the sheer cliffs of the Himalayas
   (d) wrote a letter to the United Nations which had helped bring about peace talks in a major world trouble spot
   (e) people disbelieve them
   (f) a loud voice so even people she wasn't talking to could hear
   (g) Umpire State Building
   (h) De Vorzon Superstore
   (i) ground floor   (j) fiftieth
   (k) she does not say   (l) dust mites
   (m) none
   (n) jumped out of a window
3. Phyllis does not say which floor she was on when the fire took place. She was obviously on the ground floor.
4. (a) negotiation – discussion aimed at reaching an agreement
   (b) indignant – showing anger or annoyance at being treated unfairly

The Insurance Claim .... Pages 12 – 13
1. (a) hourglass   (b) wristwatch
   (c) sundial
2. (a) New York City   (b) The Big Apple
   (c) 20 degrees below zero/very cold
   (d) We Never Pay Insurance Company
   (e) there was an insurance claim
   (f) an expensive watch
   (g) Loren's friend/an unemployed television weather reporter
   (h) $20 000
   (i) Elmo's Supermarket
   (j) Stacey Pickett   (k) Rolloff
   (l) won at the races
   (m) the duck pond in the park
   (n) it sank and disappeared in the mud
3. 100°C = boiling point of water
   37°C = healthy body temperature
   28°C = temperature on a hot summer's day
   3°C = temperature on a cold winter's day
   0°C = freezing point of water
4. The water in the duck pond would be frozen at 20° below zero. The watch couldn't sink into the mud.

Charming Beauregarde.... Pages 14 – 15

1. to search for something concealed in clothing
2. (a) ill-mannered, lazy, oafish, self-centred, a worry to his parents, a nuisance
    (b) work and save up money
    (c) steal it
    (d) baseball cap, tracksuit, trainers
    (e) in her shopping trolley
    (f) her purse
    (g) under his baseball cap
    (h) closing the store/a line-up
    (i) he'd had on a pair of sunglasses at the time he had stolen the purse/didn't want to appear suspicious
    (j) so Mrs Plum would think it couldn't possibly be him because he was so charming
    (k) lifted his cap to her
    (l) she didn't get a good enough look at the suspect
3. In trying to be overly polite and charming, he'd lifted his cap to Mrs Plum, revealing her purse underneath it.

Where's the Heir? .... Pages 16 – 17

1. intestate – not having made a will before one dies
2. heir – a person entitled to the property or rank of another on that person's death
3. (a) a person who hoards wealth and spends as little money as possible
    (b) Angus MacGurgle's heir
    (c) Scotland
    (d) Australia   (e) Mac
    (f) a trip to Scotland
    (g) Gupta MacDivot
    (h) MacHinery
    (i) Fleegle's Machine Factory
    (j) motors and machines
    (k) they had been closed down over Christmas
    (l) macwhirter, macdivot, machinery
4. MacHinery did not exist. It was a typographical error. Someone had hit upper case 'h' to turn 'machinery' into the mystery person, 'MacHinery'.
5. – 6. macaroni – a type of pasta
    macaroon – a light, sweet biscuit
    mackerel – a type of fish
    Macrocarpa – a tree with lemon-scented leaves
    macrocosm – the universe
    macushla – Irish term of endearment
    macrame – the art of tying decorative knots

Nuisance Call.................. Pages 18 – 19

1. hoax – a trick or practical joke
2. (a) Meg Burrows, PC Webber, PC Cox, the chief
    (b) the prowler
    (c) a prowler was in her garden
    (d) hoax
    (e) six months earlier at the supermarket
    (f) she'd fainted
    (g) Meg kept ringing him
    (h) wanted her to leave him alone
    (i) angry
    (j) use any breach of law you can find to punish her
    (k) 9.00 p.m.   (l) too scared
    (m) 12 hours
3. a claim that someone has done something illegal
4. It has not been proved that the person has committed the crime.
5. The battery would be flat if the lights were left on for 12 hours with the motor switched off. Meg said she started her car up straight away and drove into her garage.

Innocent or Guilty? .... Pages 20 – 21

1. fraud – criminal deception for the purpose of financial gain
2. legitimate – conforming to the law
3. (a) he thought he was going to jail for burglary
    (b) he hadn't been involved in criminal activities
    (c) stern   (d) theft, burglary
    (e) to make a fraudulent insurance claim
    (f) 2.00 a.m. on a Tuesday morning
    (g) the burglar had cut off the power
    (h) a safety match   (i) on the wall
    (j) they'd spent three years together in jail
    (k) Kristine Hall – his fiancee
4. Matches which ignite only when struck on a specially prepared surface, usually the side of a matchbox.
5. Butling said that he'd struck safety matches on the wall.
6. a public official who institutes legal proceedings against someone

The Jilted Lover............... Pages 22 – 23

1. gingerly – with great care
2. (a) two weeks
    (b) banging on doors and windows
    (c) on the city outskirts
    (d) a mess/building materials lying around
    (e) workshed; pailing fence; cement slab for carport
    (f) Mills's foot sank to ankle depth in the mud.
    (g) grubby, unshaven
    (h) pouring the concrete slab for the carport
    (i) raining
3. It had been raining for two weeks. Concrete is not poured when it is raining.
4. harassment – repeatedly making aggressive attacks
5. motive – a strong reason for doing something

Happy Holidays............... Pages 24 – 25

1. (a) Western Australia   (b) Broome
    (c) insurance money
    (d) the difference between the high and low water marks is several metres
    (e) feeding on creatures left revealed by the fallen tide
    (f) he'd been roughed up/shop burnt down
    (g) the price of the fraud is passed on to customers meaning an increased price for insurance
    (h) low
    (i) a cement block used for anchoring buoys
    (j) half a metre   (k) 15 hours
    (l) an old iron anchor piece
    (m) two kilometres
    (n) nothing/a rest in jail
2. The tides in the region rise several metres from the low water mark. The concrete block was at the water's edge at low tide and Mitchell claimed he'd been chained to it with a chain about half a metre long. He'd been unconscious for fifteen hours so, in that time there must have been a high tide. If this were true he would have drowned.
3. (a) dramatically   (b) ruin
    (c) artichoke   (d) complex
    (e) temporarily   (f) prise
    (g) exposed

Prim-Ed Publishing   www.prim-ed.com

The Kidnapped Kidnapper .... Pages 26 – 27

1. (a) hot, sunny
   (b) wastrel, spendthrift
   (c) oil
   (d) He wanted him to work through the ranks so he'd have a thorough understanding of the job and be a worthy successor.
   (e) he wanted to have fun
   (f) a lock of Gregor's hair
   (g) three days
   (h) seriously hurt
   (i) a hundred   (j) blond
   (k) blue   (l) pale
   (m) seemed quite relaxed
   (n) they'd been successful and would do the same thing again
   (o) he was blindfolded
   (p) iron stake or pole
   (q) in an open paddock
   (r) gagged him
   (s) left food and water
   (t) in front of Police Headquarters
2. Gregor said he'd been tied to a stake in an open paddock for many hours. The kidnappers removed his shirt. He is described as having pale skin. If he'd been tied up as claimed, exposure to the sun would have caused severe sunburn.

Sir Marvo the Dull .... Pages 28 – 29

1. again, aim, can, gain, gin, magi, magic, man, main, nag etc.
2. (a) the world's least interesting
   (b) ball
   (c) throw it   (d) return to him
   (e) down   (f) up
   (g) up in the air
   (h) a pistol, a hat   (i) hat
   (j) pistol
   (k) blindfold Sir Marvo, take the hat, hang it up somewhere
   (l) fifty
   (m) stop, turn and shoot a bullet straight through the hat
   (n) no
   (o) placed it on top of Sir Marvo's pistol
3. Teacher check
4. Interesting – fascinating, exciting, absorbing, engrossing
   Dull – tiresome, boring, ennui, tedious, painstaking, laborious

Inside Job .... Pages 30 – 31

1. in, win, wing, view, inter, interview, viewing
2. (a) Fitzpatrick's Jewellery Shop
   (b) Policewoman Jessica Davies, Constable Shaun Roberts
   (c) a crime committed by someone working on the premises where it occurred
   (d) Albert Fitzpatrick, Pete Moss
   (e) diamonds
   (f) sapphires, rubies, emeralds, gold
   (g) nothing smashed, safe opened without explosives
   (h) Mr Fitzpatrick, Pete Moss
   (i) on holiday
   (j) no-one
   (k) Wilbur Lawrence
   (l) what had been taken
   (m) diamonds
   (n) he was in jail
3. Lawrence supposedly knew nothing about the robbery but knew that they were looking for a diamond thief.
4. (a) amethyst   (b) ruby
   (c) emerald   (d) sapphire
   (e) diamond

Crooks Never Prosper ...... Pages 32 – 33

1. (a) getaway car driver
   (b) a hot day
   (c) close to half an hour
   (d) 'Ferret'
   (e) he was pushing it rather than pulling it
   (f) on the car's back seat
   (g) put the car under cover in his lockup garage
   (h) laughed, gave each other 'high fives' and punched each other in the shoulder
   (i) a minute later
   (j) return some car parts
   (k) beautifully polished
   (l) a grub
   (m) to feel the glossy paintwork
   (n) pulled his hand away sharply
   (o) in the garage
   (p) criminals get away with crimes/live well on the takings
   (q) didn't think the car had been inside all morning
   (r) serving lengthy stretches in jail for armed robbery
2. It had been a hot day. Because of this and the fact that it had just sped from the hold-up, the car was hot to touch. Santini became aware of this when he went to feel its glossy paintwork. When the robbers told him that the car had been in the garage all morning, Santini knew that they were lying. It was this lie that aroused his suspicion and made him want to have a closer look.
3. Teacher check

Late Again .... Pages 34 – 35

1. (a) early   (b) late
   (c) on time
2. (a) bellhop
   (b) Walford Gastoria Hotel
   (c) showing visitors to their rooms; carrying visitors luggage; supplying needs for room service
   (d) crisp navy blue trousers; navy blue jacket with gold trimming; choice of either navy blue or black socks
   (e) Mr Silverstein
   (f) Jeremy was often late for work.
   (g) someone had to do his job as well as their own
   (h) three-quarters of an hour
   (i) it became stuck
   (j) one at a time   (k) twenty
   (l) ten   (m) eleven
   (n) miss the bus
3. His uniform allowed him to wear either blue or black socks. He said that he had to pull out eleven socks before he had a pair the same colour. He would have had a pair the same colour after pulling out a maximum of three socks.
4. (a) concierge – a hotel's caretaker
   (b) dumb waiter – a small lift for carrying things such as food and crockery between the floors of a building

Bad Day for Bobby .... Pages 36 – 37

1. (a) Mercedes
   (b) burned it to get some insurance money
   (c) Powell's statement
   (d) Monday, 22 January, 2006
   (e) the day before this statement
   (f) typed letters, answered emails
   (g) post office   (h) bank
   (i) about two streets away
   (j) he'd forgotten some papers there
   (k) took his wife's car to look for his allegedly stolen Mercedes
   (l) on a deserted road on the city outskirts near the dump
   (m) a pair of scissors   (n) cheat
   (o) his wife's jewellery
   (p) making number plates for other people's expensive cars
2. Powell's statement is dated Monday 22 January. In it, he refers to the events happening 'yesterday'. As the day before Monday is Sunday he would not have been able to buy stamps at the Post Office nor carry out his banking. On Sundays post offices and banks are shut.
3. Teacher check
4. Teacher check